MAJOR-LEAGUE
Batboy

MAJOR-LEAGUE Batboy

CHUCK SOLOMON

CROWN PUBLISHERS, INC., NEW YORK

The author would like to thank Anthony Pastore, Frank Coppenbarger,
Larry Shenk, Tina Urban, and the players, coaches, and fans of the
Philadelphia Phillies.

Published by Crown Publishers, Inc., a Random House company,
225 Park Avenue South, New York, New York 10003
CROWN is a trademark of Crown Publishers, Inc.
Manufactured in Hong Kong

Library of Congress Cataloging-in-Publication Data
Solomon, Chuck. Major-League Batboy/Chuck Solomon. p. cm.
Summary: Text and photographs follow a day in the life of a batboy
for a major league baseball team. 1. Baseball—Pictorial works—
Juvenile literature (1. Baseball.) I. Title.
GV867.5.S64 1991   796.357'022'2—dc20   90-43275 CIP AC
ISBN 0-517-58244-9 (trade)
ISBN 0-517-58245-7 (lib. bdg.)

10 9 8 7 6 5 4 3 2 1

First Edition

When you're a batboy in the major leagues, it's like being part of the team.

At game time, you put on a uniform and go down to the dugout with the players. Your job is to take care of the bats and playing equipment and to keep the dugout tidy. It's a thrill to step out onto the floodlit field while cheering fans fill the seats and the announcer calls out the lineups.

But you also work off the field, in the clubhouse, where the players and coaches prepare for the game. Being a batboy takes you behind the scenes of major-league baseball.

When your team is playing at home, you
get to work early: five or six hours before
game time. The clubhouse is beneath the
seats behind first base. There's a locker room,
with a locker for each player. There are also
showers, offices for the manager and the
coaches, a workout room, and a trainer's
room.

There's a locker for you, too; above it there's
a nameplate that says "Batboy."

The equipment manager explains the day's chores.

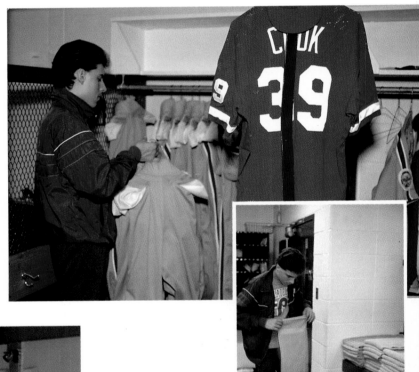

Clean uniforms and towels must be put in each player's locker.

The shower is checked to make sure there's enough soap and shampoo.

Players like to snack.
You put out candy,
chips, and fruit,
and make drinks.

Usually, there's a
big pile of mail,
so you sort it
into the players'
mailboxes.

Meanwhile, the players
begin to arrive. They take
showers and change into
their pregame uniforms,
which are a different color
and design from their
official playing uniforms.
Some go to the trainer's
room for exercises or a
massage. Others go to the
workout room.

A batboy helps take care of
playing equipment. Shoes
must be cleaned every day—
forty pairs! Every few days, the
team's batting helmets have
to be polished.

Major-league hitters use as many as
seventy or eighty bats in a season, so plenty
of spares are kept on hand in the clubhouse.
Most bats are made from the wood of ash
trees, which is strong but light.
The bats are individually made
for each player in a comfortable
weight and length, and are
numbered so they don't get
mixed up.

There's a lot to do, but
between jobs there's time to
have lunch and keep up with
schoolwork. The batboy usually
doesn't travel with the team,
so when the team is on the
road, you get some time off.

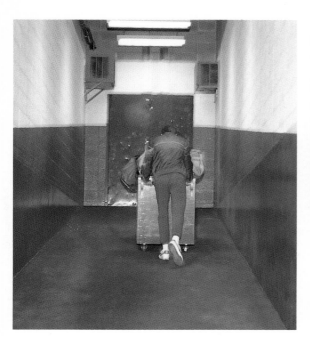

Before every game, the team takes batting practice, and it's the batboy's job to take the equipment down to the field. You push a big cart loaded with bats along the runway from the clubhouse to the dugout and carry out the equipment bags full of helmets and gloves.

There are cubbyholes
in the dugout, where
the players' helmets
and batting gloves are
kept during the game.
Some players also use
shin guards to protect
their legs from foul balls or
thumb guards to protect
their hands. You make sure
everything is in its place,
ready for use.

To get a good grip on the bat, hitters use a gooey liquid called pine tar. They rub the handle of the bat with a rag loaded with pine tar, then dust it off with a white powder called rosin. It's your job to soak the rags with pine tar from a can and to make sure the rosin bag is full.

The team divides into groups for batting practice. One group hits in the batting cage, watched by the hitting instructor.

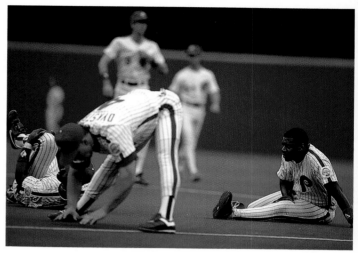

The others do stretching exercises and go out to field. Infielders practice fielding ground balls and turning double plays; outfielders catch fly balls in the outfield. Meanwhile, fans who have come early to the game ask for autographs.

It's great to see the players at work from close up. You can learn a lot about the game by watching and talking to them.

After batting practice the players change into uniforms and get ready for the game. They prepare their gloves. Some rub them with oil; others use shaving cream to soften them and make them flexible. A few hitters like to customize their bats by shaving the handles. This makes them thinner and whippier, and may deliver a fraction more power when the ball is hit.

One of the clubhouse staff prepares the official game balls by rubbing them with a special kind of mud taken from the Delaware River. This discolors them and makes them less slick, so the pitcher can get a better grip.

It's almost game time.
You put on your uniform
and go down to the dugout.
You take fresh towels, gum
and seeds for the players to
chew during the game,
and drums full of ice water
and thirst-quenching
drinks.

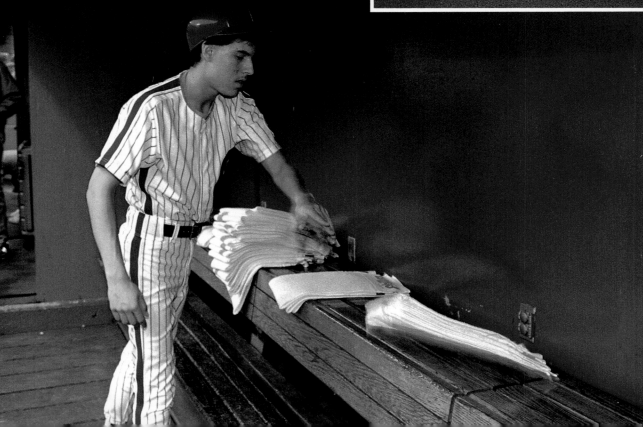

Out on the field, the ground crew dismantles the batting cage. They put a fresh coat of paint on home plate and mark new lines around the batter's box.

The base paths and the pitcher's mound are watered to keep the dust down.

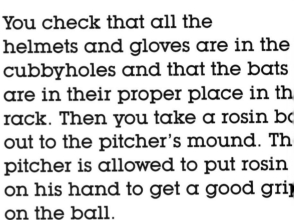

You check that all the helmets and gloves are in the cubbyholes and that the bats are in their proper place in th rack. Then you take a rosin bc out to the pitcher's mound. Th pitcher is allowed to put rosin on his hand to get a good grip on the ball.

The national anthem is sun

The four umpires gather at home plate, and
the team managers bring out the lineup cards.
The first pitch is thrown and the game begins.

Because it's a home game, your team comes up to bat in the bottom half of the inning. You carry the batting equipment out to the on-deck circle, where the hitters wait for their turn to bat. There are special weighted bats and doughnut-shaped weights that fit around an ordinary bat. The hitters use these to help them loosen up before they face the opposing pitcher. After a few practice swings with a weighted bat, a regular bat feels light and easy to swing. There's also a pine-tar rag and a rosin bag for hitters to use on their bat handles.

Today, the first batter strikes out. On his way back to the dugout, he tosses his bat and helmet to the ground, and you pick them up and put them away, so that they're ready for his next time up.

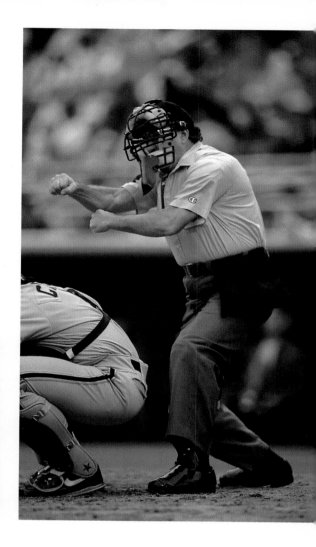

The next man up gets a hit. You run out to the batter's box to collect his bat, then out to first base to get his shin guard.

It's important for a batboy to watch the game carefully. A foul ball lands behind home plate, so you run out and pick it up. A moment later, the home plate umpire runs out of balls. He signals, telling you how many he needs, and you carry them out to him. Then the pitcher is up to bat. You find his jacket in the dugout: it is a cool day, and if he gets on base, he will need it to keep his throwing arm warm.

You must work quickly so that play is not interrupted. The game goes well. Batters hit safely and steal bases. Runs score and soon your team's ahead. In the field, they play good defense and protect the lead.

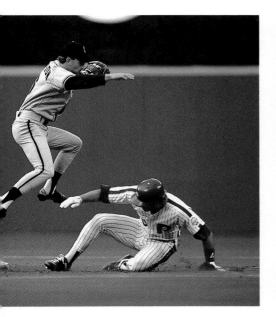

The dugout is a great place to watch the action. A close play at home plate or a long ball hit deep toward the outfield fence brings the crowd to its feet and fills the stadium with cheers.

Before long, the last out has been made
and the game is over. The players go back to
the clubhouse to shower
and talk to reporters, but
you stay behind in the
dugout. Towels and empty
drink drums must be
collected and taken back
to the clubhouse.

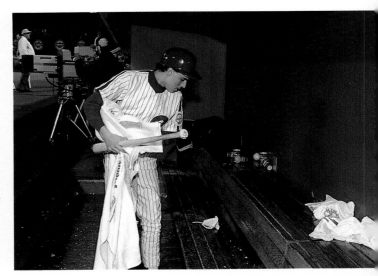

While one member of the team gives a postgame radio interview, you pack all the helmets and gloves into the equipment bags and put the bats back into the cart.

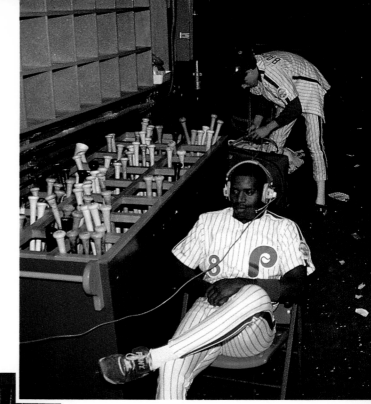

Outside the dugout, the lights have been
switched off and the stadium is quiet after the
noise and excitement of the game. Tomorrow
the fans will be back, the teams will battle
each other again, and you will be here,
doing your job in the clubhouse and on the
field.